Understanding SECURITY choice

TRUST

B·A·L·A·N·C·E LOVE WARMTH

Happiness Accord Blessing

Freedom TRANQUILLITY

MATURITY peace SURPRISE!

harmony

Zest cheer

JOY CALM life Enthusiasm

HONOUR

BLISS

comfort pleasure Delight QUIET

FRESHNESS TENDERNESS

Laughter GROWTH fruition

HEALTH sunshine

Text copyright © 1994 Jean Watson
Illustrations copyright © Jane Hughes 1994
This edition © 1994 Lion Publishing

The author asserts the moral right
to be identified as the author of this work

Published by
Lion Publishing plc
Sandy Lane West, Oxford, England
ISBN 0 7459 2837 4
Albatross Books Pty Ltd
PO Box 320, Sutherland, NSW 2232, Australia
ISBN 0 7324 0863 6

First edition 1994

A catalogue record for this book is available
from the British Library

Library of Congress CIP Data applied for

Calligraphy by Gillian Hazeldine

Printed and bound in Singapore

The Spirit of

PEACE

in a busy world

JEAN WATSON

Illustrated by
Jane Hughes

A LION BOOK

INTRODUCTION

Little Daniel was being read the story of Pilgrim's Progress. *One bedtime, after the part about Apollyon and Christian, he prayed, 'O God, make the baddie Apollyon good.' Then came a pause before he added a perceptive postscript: 'But not too good, or it'll spoil the story!'*

Though young, he had already realized that conflict and difficulty are essential in a good, gripping tale. They make the final resolution even more welcome and satisfying, requiring the hero or heroine to reach great heights of bravery and resourcefulness before winning through.

The aftermath or afterglow of successful struggle is a hard-won, happy form of peace. Artists in any field certainly experience something of this, but all sorts of other enterprises can also bring us to the place where we can enjoy relief and satisfaction.

And more tangible sources of peace lie all around us, like loving gifts. If, for example, we are frequently confronted by dirt and ugliness, bombarded by noise and pressurized into constant activity, the beauty, tranquillity and freshness of the countryside may be just the peaceful break we need.

But without peace 'inside', it is difficult to benefit fully from peace 'outside', let alone relate harmoniously to one another. And for me, deep inner ease and wholeness is linked with God's peace. Like the still centre of the eye of a hurricane, it exists in the midst of — and despite — all sorts of surrounding disturbance. And like yeast, it's active, an agent for change: profound and subtle peace — much needed, not just because it enhances the present quality of our lives, but also because, coming from God, it inspires in us a powerful hope for future peace.

Whatever aspects of peace you most need at this time, I hope with all my heart that this book will help you to take hold of them or let them take hold of you.

Jean Watson

A QUIET INNER CENTRE

In William Golding's novel *The Paper Men*, I came across this thumbnail sketch of a minor character in the story:

'She had a kind of security – that kind which stems perhaps from getting on very well without some of our less attractive qualities, such as the need for revenge, more success than other people, protection from other people or indifference to them . . . I remember ending our time together envying her bitterly. The things you could see that woman had no need of!'

Such people are not necessarily placid by temperament; nor are they lazy and uncaring. But they do, in a sense, not care overmuch about 'what teacher says' or what the 'Joneses next door' possess. They are free from addiction and self-obsessed competitiveness; from knee-jerk reactions, crippling anxieties and fears.

This inner peace comes through knowing and valuing ourselves, because we are known and valued by others, and by God. And so we are able to grow in this security, and to help others in their growth as well. As we offer a listening ear, and a quiet heart, to some of the driven people around us, they too can find release, and grow in their inner security.

A man or woman who has developed . . . solitude of heart is no longer pulled apart by the most divergent stimuli of the surrounding world, but is able to perceive and understand this world from a quiet inner centre.

Henri Nouwen

. . . you were called to be free. But do not let this freedom become an excuse for letting your physical desires control you. Instead, let love make you serve one another.

From Galatians 5

TIME ALONE

Someone told me that when she's on her own, surrounded by peace and quiet, she has to create some sort of noise and bustle. I made a joke about her not liking her own company and she did a slight double-take before giving a light-hearted reply.

Why does privacy feel so threatening at times? Is it because, in the absence of distractions, we feel empty, weary, frightened, lost or lonely? Or are we suddenly aware of memories, obligations, or whatever it is we've been repressing or trying to block out through frantic busyness?

I've certainly been there. But I've found that if I can bear the feelings, or be helped to stay with them, and deal with my inner unease instead of running away or creating some distraction, I don't regret it. Because through this comes peace. As things ease up inside, I am able once more to enjoy quiet, private pursuits – walks, listening to music, leafing through a much-loved book – and these, in turn, promote a deeper inner calm.

Privacy, wherever and however we find it, provides a balance for busy people leading busy, sociable lives. It offers a context in which we can take stock, gain new insights and be more imaginative and creative. In private, we can study, pray, keep a journal, or practise a craft. So we grow in wisdom and skill, and have more to offer. We also grow in inner peace, and are far more able to listen – in all senses of the word – to others.

I will think about all that you have done.

From Psalm 77

Artists, like inventors, seem to need the elbow-room
of tense leisure to produce a drama, a novel, a concerto
or a poem.

Calvin Seerveld

A life all turbulence and noise may seem
To him that leads it wise and to be praised,
But wisdom is a pearl with most success
Sought in still waters.

William Cowper

THE FRUITS OF SOLITUDE

Privacy helps us to develop solitude – a capacity for inner aloneness, as distinct from loneliness. Solitude is necessary to 'listening' in depth – to our past perhaps in particular, to our present routines and use of time, to our thoughts and feelings, moods and attitudes, to our relationships and needs, and to our bodies and perhaps our dreams.

I once heard of an extrovert and gregarious person who had lost a son by cot death. Apparently, every so often, he would shut himself away and play on the piano a particular tune which reminded him of his son. Most people knew him as a comedian, but his wife always said that these were his times of greatest strength.

It is often in solitude that pennies start to drop and confusion begins to clear. We hear, at last, what God has been whispering to us, or what our own hearts or others have been trying to tell us. We grasp the connection between our present reactions and some incident, fear or feeling from the past. We can see beyond appearances to deeper realities . . .

Introspection as an end in itself becomes sterile and unsatisfying. But genuine solitude is nothing like that. And if we involve God in our inner garden, then the tree of solitude will produce some of the best fruit, both for ourselves and for others.

After the fire, there was the soft whisper of a voice.

From 1 Kings 19

A lonely person has no inner time nor inner rest to wait and listen. He wants answers and wants them here and now. But in solitude we can pay attention to our inner self. This has nothing to do with egocentrism or unhealthy introspection.

Henri Nouwen

It is in deep solitude that I find the gentleness with which I can truly love my brothers. The more solitary I am, the more affection I have for them. It is pure affection and filled with reverence for the solitudes of others.

Thomas Merton

UNITY WITHIN

Peace is not just the absence of war or other disturbances. Nor is it passive and insipid. In its fullest sense, it is active and dynamic. I like the Hebrew word for it, which is *shalom*. It means wholeness in every area of life – well-being that leads to well-doing.

Such peace stems from inner integration around a suitable purpose; from knowing and being at peace about who we are and where we're going, and from unity and harmony of mind, will, emotion and spirit.

Sometimes people focus their lives around something that proves unsuitable and unsatisfactory – the fruit-machine scenario. Others veer between trying to meet other people's expectations and their own ideals and wishes: 'I'm going to be a doctor – it's what my parents want . . .', 'I must be nice, then people will like me . . .'. The outcome either way is likely to be unsatisfactory and disappointing. It may even cause some to take refuge in the false peace of lethargy, fatalism or despair.

But there is a different option: one that sets us free to hold realism and hope together. It involves integrating our lives around God's standards and purposes for human beings and the world. This takes account both of our potential and of our imperfections, and gives us the resources to overcome the latter – growing into more harmonious, whole, co-ordinated and purposeful human beings.

Come to me, all of you who are tired from carrying heavy loads, and I will give you rest. Take my yoke and put it on you . . . For the yoke I will give you is easy, and the load I will put on you is light.

From Matthew 11

The Lord is my pace-setter, I shall not rush . . .
He leads me in the way of efficiency,
through calmness of mind;
and his guidance is peace.

Toki Miyushina

AT HOME

I heard a psychiatrist say that the happiest, best-adjusted people are those who are equally 'at home' alone and in company. And there's an overlap between being at ease in both contexts.

One woman I know avoided socializing because she was terrified that people would ask her how her first husband had died. She needed, and fortunately found, someone she trusted with whom she was able to face the facts – and more importantly the feelings – about her husband's death. In this way, she became at home to herself and therefore more ready to warm to others.

Another instance came at a conference at which I was speaking about the imagination. A woman invited me to her room and pulled out of hiding a story she was writing, with the words, 'I daren't show this to anyone at my church, because we're taught that stories are lies and must therefore be wrong.' Leaving aside this appalling misconception about fact and truth, here was someone who was receiving a pretty worthless form of acceptance because she was having to 'edit out' aspects of her true self for fear of rejection.

To be at home to ourselves, we need to be known, accepted and understood as we are, by human beings and – at very much deeper levels – by God. This sets us free to change. We are able to deal with true or false guilt and shame, and any hold our secrets may have over us. We become truly 'at home' to peace, and peace will find its own home in us.

Acceptance means that though there is need for growth, I am not forced. I do not have to be the person I am not. Acceptance liberates everything in me. Only when I am loved in that deep sense of complete acceptance, can I become myself.

Peter van Breeman

It is as we listen to ourselves in the context of the God who made us that we discover our deepest identity . . . I am most fully myself when I find myself in God.

Anne Long

I stand at the door and knock; if anyone hears my voice and opens the door, I will come into his house and eat with him, and he will eat with me.

From Revelation 3

IDENTITY

There is a scene in a recent film in which a woman is propositioned by a married man. When she refuses his attentions, he asks her if it is because she is scared. She replies, 'No. I don't want to because I'm married. I know who I am.'

If we do not know who we are, we will be unstable and make erratic decisions. To be real with ourselves, we need to become aware of our thoughts and feelings, our needs and wants, our strengths and weaknesses. Knowing and accepting ourselves is the crucial basis for a strong sense of identity.

Of course, some forms of so-called self-acceptance smack of arrogance; they say in effect: 'I'm OK. I don't want to change and if you don't like it, you can lump it.' But such attitudes are not the genuine article. True self-acceptance says something more along the lines of: 'This is me for now, but I'm aware of my imperfections and immaturity, and I'm willing to change.'

A willingness to change, paradoxical as this may sound, is the mark of someone with a *strong* sense of identity. On the other hand, a weak sense of identity shows in a fear of change. Through love and acceptance from family, friends and God, we can let go of defensive attitudes and begin to grow into a true sense of ourselves.

Perfect love drives out all fear.

From 1 John 4

True humility is an authentic appreciation of ourselves
in a way that neither exaggerates nor underestimates
what we are.

Jack Dominian

[Identity] is found in living in the midst of a constantly
changing inner and outer world and growing in a sense of
peace with oneself, with God, and with other people . . . a
continual process of housecleaning, consolidation and
reorganisation.

Dick Keyes

HOSPITALITY

'No one can be a good host who is not at home in his own house.'
Esther de Waal

If we are not 'at home' to ourselves, we are not able to put others at ease no matter how much we are offering in material terms. The first step towards being 'at home' to ourselves is to face up to unpleasant experiences and feelings. Perhaps we avoid others out of fear? Perhaps we feel superior – or inferior? Perhaps we expect too much of others and feel vulnerable to rejection? Such feelings can lead to great tension and frustration.

A welcoming home on the other hand is one where we accept others for themselves, not for what we have been given as hosts. Hospitality is when we *enjoy* being open to others. Fortunately, this usually means that others are open to us in return!

Hospitality of heart, which blesses both giver and receiver, is about self-giving, not self-display, and is based on consideration for the other's needs and wishes. Time and tangible offerings are valuable and valued – a hot drink, a meal, the give and take of genuine conversation. What they express and convey are genuine love, respect and acceptance; what they bring are understanding and peace.

. . . Nothing remains so true
As the outgoingness. This moving house
Is home, and my home, only when it's shared.

C. Day Lewis

Providing a free and empty space for others, we commit
ourselves to accepting the strangeness of strangers. Each
brings a gift, themselves. In our openness, we are
challenged by each guest, changed by them unpredictably.

Graeme L. Chapman

I was hungry and you fed me . . . I was a stranger and you
received me in your homes . . . I was sick and you took care
of me . . . Whenever you did this for one of the least
important of these brothers of mine, you did it for me.

From Matthew 25

REST AND RESTORATION

We hear a great deal about the damage caused by stress. But it can help athletes to run their best, students to study hard and pass exams well, and artists to achieve excellence – provided, of course, that the pressure is not too great, and they give themselves a good balance of rest and relaxation.

But some forms of stress are not so healthy – frustration at not being able to do what we want to do and are capable of. People longing for work, or in unsuitable work, know all about that.

We all need rest and restoration but find it in different ways. Some people find that simple, everyday experiences help them to unwind: having a nap, looking at trees, fixing a bike, even doing the washing-up. Others like to try something new, to solve a puzzle, to let their minds play and exercise their imagination.

Perhaps holding a happy baby, laughing at a silly radio sketch, or reading a magazine – anything can help us unwind. Then we can celebrate life's joys and be compassionate and hopeful about its sufferings.

All manner of small things can bring that sense of peacefulness when we are really relaxed. Then, and possibly only then, we are fully equipped to start being active again.

Let us go off by ourselves to some place where we will
be alone and you can rest for a while.

From Mark 6

You will break the bow if you always keep it bent.

Old Greek motto

Frodo was now safe in the Last Homely House east of
the Sea. That house was, as Bilbo had long ago reported,
'a perfect house, whether you like food or sleep or story-
telling or singing, or just sitting and thinking best, or a
pleasant mixture of them all'. Merely to be there was a
cure for weariness, fear, and sadness.

***The Lord of the Rings*, J.R.R. Tolkien**

CHECKING OUT ATTITUDES

Peace-friendly attitudes	Anti-peace attitudes
ready to listen	wanting to hold the floor
open to new ideas	closed mind, prejudging
'I could be wrong.'	'I'm right and you'd better believe it!'
conciliatory, gentle, relaxed	prickly, pugnacious, combative
quietly assertive, if necessary	dogmatic, explosive
patient, consistent	impatient, erratic
friendly, open, supportive	hostile, defensive, aggressive
seeking truth	desperate to win the argument
working to restore harmony	wanting to humiliate others
enjoying closeness and stillness	fearing closeness and stillness

Peace-friendly attitudes	Anti-peace attitudes
purposeful, orderly	frenetic, haphazard
willing to change	opposed to change
able to be spontaneous	rigid
self-controlled, self-determined	obsessional, addictive, driven
able to laugh and have fun	tense, strained
prepared to be vulnerable	scared of being found out
enjoying solitude and company	uneasy alone and with others
open to God, self and others	full of 'no go' areas
resourceful, imaginative	panicky, threatened
willing to trust, but not naively	distrustful or gullible
room for variety	inflexible

GREEN PEACE

The sheer beauty of nature – forests, seas, flowers – is reason enough to treasure it. But we also depend upon nature for our very survival and its resources must be managed so that life's quality, or even life itself, is preserved.

Some aspects of nature, such as earthquakes and floods, are terrifying. Often unpredictable, they can cause untold destruction. But our inhumanity to one another and to the environment is even more horrifying in view of our intellectual, spiritual and physical capacities to alleviate distress.

There *are* ways in which we can manage the earth's resources better. Something this important can't be left to 'them in charge'. We're all part of the problem and we should all be part of the answer. For instance, we can take care about how we dispose of our waste; we may be able to mend and maintain our machines instead of buying new ones; we can be more efficient in our use of electricity and gas in the home, or transport in the community; we could perhaps become involved in pressure groups.

The earth is part of God's extravagant and imaginative generosity towards us. It is up to us to appreciate it to the full and, one way or another, help to take the best possible care of it. And when we do, it becomes a deep source of joy and peace to us, and also to its future tenants.

Lord, you have made so many things!
How wisely you made them all!

From Psalm 104

Earth is the Lord's: it is ours to enjoy it,
Ours, as his stewards, to farm and defend.
From its pollution, misuse, and destruction,
Good Lord, deliver us, world without end!

Fred Pratt Green

PUTTING THINGS RIGHT

We should feel angry at every aspect of people's inhumanity to one another. To rest easy when things are wrong indicates ignorance or lack of care.

Imagine that someone has spread malicious gossip and falsehoods about someone you are fond of. Anger may well be appropriate to the situation, and bring about positive change. But only if the anger is constructive.

Self-control, ensuring that the anger does not get out of hand or become an excuse for verbal or physical violence, is vital. So, too, are self-honesty and humility. Only as we become aware of our own failings can we listen to others properly, and be open to the possibility that we could be wrong, and they right, in whole or in part.

In particular, before confronting anyone, we need to be honest about our true objectives. What do we really want to come out of the encounter? Do we want genuine resolution and reconciliation – with everyone happy, or at least no one unhappy? Or do we want victory or credit for ourselves?

Of course, anger is often sheer bad temper or a response to hurt, rather than an outcry against injustice. So the need for honesty and forgiveness – given and received – cannot be over-emphasized. A good approach is never to 'let the sun go down' on anger – to make things up on a daily basis. But however we do it, putting things right is important: it's the vital key to lasting peace.

Hot tempers cause arguments but patience brings
peace . . . It is better to win control over yourself than over
whole cities.

From Proverbs 15; 16

I was angry with my friend:
I told my wrath, my wrath did end.

From 'A Poison Tree', William Blake

WORKING FOR PEACE

World peace is about the world's people living in community and harmony. There are many organizations working for peace and reconciliation. We can support fair trade with developing countries; we can 'adopt' a war victim in a refugee home overseas; we can, through a multitude of societies, wage war on ignorance, inequality, oppression and other enemies of peace and well-being.

But peacemaking can, and must, begin closer to home: by facing up to and dealing with our own 'them and us' attitudes. How do we react to our neighbour who votes differently from us, or to the young couple who've bought the expensive house we wanted? And what about the homeless in our town – how do we treat the people on the corner that others dismiss as 'old drunks'?

We need to stand alongside the disadvantaged and vulnerable in our homes, in our places of work and in our neighbourhoods, before we can begin to tackle oppression worldwide. Giving to aid projects in other countries does not absolve us from working at problems in our own towns and villages. We must learn to reach out to others and create a sense of community around us.

It is much more rewarding to light a small candle rather than curse the darkness. It is better to spread a few ripples of justice, peace and order than to stand back, gloomily predicting that the tide of injustice, conflict and disorder will sweep us to our doom. And if God is working in and with us, peace, order and justice will ultimately prevail.

I am only one. But I still am one.
I cannot do everything. But still I can do something.
And because I cannot do everything,
I will not refuse to do the something that I can do.

Edward Everett Hale

Happy are those who work for peace; God will call them his children.

From Matthew 5

PEACE PEOPLE

What names spring to mind when you think of great peacemakers? Abraham Lincoln, Martin Luther King, Mother Teresa, Nelson Mandela? A host of other famous people could be mentioned, and there is an even greater host of those who, though not household names, are nevertheless spreading peace around them. It's a task which requires every one of us.

There are so many ways in which we can be peace people. One of the first and most important is by learning to be good listeners – not just to what people say, but to their silences, and body language, as well. And by listening to others we will be better able to welcome strangers, or even reach out to enemies, with a view to turning them into friends; to value and support those who feel worthless, weak and inadequate, and help them grow more confident and resourceful.

Something as low-key as inviting someone to join us for a meal or an outing, making a thoughtful phone call or writing a friendly letter, can be a beginning.

You do not have to be a forceful, 'up front' sort of person in order to spread peace. In fact, the most effective peace people are often quiet, and free from the need to impress. Above all, their concern is to promote true peace – reconciliation, wholeness and well-being.

Be happy with those who are happy, weep with those who weep. Have the same concern for everyone . . . Do everything possible on your part to live in peace with everybody. Never take revenge . . .

From Romans 12

Drop thy still dews of quietness,
Till all our strivings cease;
Take from our souls the strain and stress,
And let our ordered lives confess
The beauty of thy peace.

John Greenleaf Whittier

PUTTING THE PAST TO REST

To have peace in the present, it's important to be at ease about the past. And for all of us, this involves forgiving and being forgiven. Sometimes we behave badly towards one another, and before relationships can be fully restored, there must be acknowledgment of the wrong. Then we really do have to say – and mean – 'sorry', and to forgive any hurt caused.

Humility and vulnerability go right against the image of the super-cool, self-sufficient types who do it their way, regret nothing and need no one. But an admission of frailty may be an indication of true strength, and can lead to genuine and lasting peace. We are then able to receive forgiveness from God and other people – and so to forgive ourselves. And all that overflows into our relationships and lifestyle.

This process is not easy. As Adlai Stevenson said, 'We must have patience – making peace is harder than making war.' But it's far better than pretending that all is well while having to make sure our 'skeletons' from the past are locked away, out of sight; or living in an atmosphere of unresolved conflict and grudges. And the joy that follows makes all the pain and effort worthwhile.

Perhaps we should take our cue from children in this. More readily than the rest of us, they are willing to forget past insults, and put another building-block in place!

Without feelings of guilt, humanity is brutalised;
without forgiveness and compassion, the consequences
can be lethal.

Jack Dominian

When I did not confess my sins, I was worn out from crying
all day long . . . Then I confessed my sins to you . . . and you
forgave all my sins.

From Psalm 32

Or what is else? There is your world within.
There rid the dragons, root out there the sin.
Your will is law in that small commonweal.

Gerard Manley Hopkins

THE PRESENT

Peace on a day-to-day basis involves asking the right things of ourselves, and then quietly getting on with them. But what are these 'right things'?

Some people make lists every day, and have the satisfaction of ticking each item as they complete each task. That's all right as far as it goes – but very often such lists focus on the urgent at the expense of the important.

They tend not to include things like the following, for example: *Hug baby a lot. Be free to listen to J when he gets back. Walk. Stare at the clouds. Smell the flowers. Give some thought to X. Pray. Make a decision about Y. Make cake with my grandchild.*

Yet these things may be closer to important priorities: the things we really should be asking of ourselves on a daily basis rather than – or at least as well as – buying deodorant, cleaning the car, and so on.

Asking the right things of ourselves also means asking what we can manage. We need to be aware of our resources, of our age and stage in life. Do you see your present situation – job, home, looks – and feel frustrated? Do you waste time in futile guilt? Or do you focus instead on enjoying what can be enjoyed and on changing what can and should be changed?

If we ask the right things of ourselves and others, we will be able to focus on what is important and good and possible, day by day. That way, we will begin to experience real peace and a harmony within our lives.

True contentment is the power of getting out of any situation all that there is in it.

G.K. Chesterton

Freedom and a country where he could live in safety: David wanted both. 'But nothing more,' he told himself. 'Just those two things and that will be enough. Johannes said that greedy people can never be happy and I would so much like to know what it feels like to be happy.'

I Am David, **Anne Holm**

. . . the Lord has told us what is good. What he requires of us is this: to do what is just, to show constant love, and to live in humble fellowship with our God.

From Micah 6

LOOKING AHEAD

One of my teachers used to quote what I thought was a very pessimistic phrase, 'As now, so then'. Often when we're young we expect some wonderful future event to change us or our lives completely. 'Things will be different when I'm married . . . when we have children . . . after a holiday . . . when I stop working . . . ' But as life goes on, we discover that real change usually takes a long time, and one 'magic' event isn't enough to bring it about.

The future may well bring us unexpected events and new situations. But the significant milestones will relate to what is happening to us now, the fruition of past events – the birth of a child or grandchild; the successful completion of years of training; a wedding anniversary; a sporting or artistic achievement.

But it isn't just what we do and have done which shapes the future. It's also our overall perspective – how we see the past, present and future. It makes sense to see them as a whole, each one affecting the others in all sorts of ways.

And as far as the future is concerned, much depends on whether we see life in the context of eternity and universal perspectives. Whatever thoughts we have, our feelings and attitudes about the future affect us in the present. And for me, what makes the future – both short- and long-term – look less frightening and more reassuring is to be able to say and believe, 'I don't know what the future holds, but I know who holds the future.'

This small and temporary trouble we suffer will bring us a tremendous and eternal glory, much greater than the trouble.

From 2 Corinthians 4

All their life in this world and all their adventures in Narnia had only been the cover and the title page: now at last they were beginning Chapter One of the Great Story which no one on earth has read: which goes on for ever: in which every chapter is better than the one before.

***The Last Battle*, C.S. Lewis**

FINDING A BALANCE

Peace has close links with order, whether we're talking about inner order or external organization. When my study is in order, I feel more peaceful. But the sort of order I am happiest with might not seem orderly at all to someone else: everything I need for a current project is to hand, but there may be books open and papers out all over the place – a kind of controlled chaos; order with loose ends!

Of course, an appearance of neatness doesn't necessarily reflect genuine order. In some homes, life seems to run smoothly with no open arguments, but resentments may be simmering just below the surface. Similarly, repressive regimes may look ordered and peaceful. But, as was evident to all in Romania a few years ago, the moment there's any relaxation of control, all hell breaks loose.

Genuinely good order incorporates openness, freedom, equality, respect, justice and fair play. It needs people committed to those ideals. We often want to be such people but we need forgiveness and help to keep developing the necessary attitudes and qualities. With God's and other people's forgiveness and help, however, good order becomes increasingly realizable personally and globally. Such good order is an aspect of 'just peace' – peace with honour – which is so wonderfully welcome at every level of interaction and transaction you can think of.

Where there is jealousy and selfishness, there is also disorder and every kind of evil.

From James 3

God is the only reality, and we are only real in so far as we are in his order, and he in us.

Augustine

With malice toward none; with charity for all: with firmness in the right, as God gives us to see the right, let us strive on to finish the work we are in . . . to do all which may achieve and cherish a just and lasting peace among ourselves, and with all nations.

Abraham Lincoln

TRUST

Peace goes hand in hand with safety. If, on a daily basis, we feel physically safe, we can go about our lives calmly. Many are not so fortunate: those living in war-torn lands, and under repressive regimes, or in areas prone to natural disasters. Unable to trust their government, those around them, or their environment, they live in fear of their lives.

But bad experiences are not confined to such places and situations. There is the story of the father who put his child on a ledge and told her to jump. When she obeyed, he failed to catch her, and so she fell. Looking down at her, he then said, 'I wanted you to learn that you can never trust anyone'!

If it were true that we could never trust anyone, we would never feel safe, and life would not be worth living. Of course, peace and safety, either physical or emotional, cannot be guaranteed to anyone in this world. Accidents, illness and so on can change life, and take away the thing or person we have been depending on.

But many people are, thank God, sufficiently trustworthy as friends, mentors, colleagues, or whatever. And we need to be like that for one another, particularly for those – like the little girl – who have been damaged. Relationships with mutual trust make life worthwhile – they can replace fear and uncertainty with confidence.

My trust is in you, O Lord . . . I am always in your care.

From Psalm 31

The analogy I like best of God's upholding is that of the singer and the song. The song depends totally on being uttered by the singer, moment by moment. So it is, I believe, with God and the universe, including mankind. We owe our moment-by-moment existence to the upholding of God.

Colin Humphreys

In his will is our peace.

Dante Alighieri

FINDING A BALANCE

None of us can feel perfect peace all the time – it would be oversimplifying life or running away from reality. I am reminded of the ironic amendment to some lines written by Kipling:

If you can keep your head when all about you
Are losing theirs . . .
Then you haven't really grasped the situation.

But that's not always the case. It is possible sometimes to remain calm, in spite of having grasped a tough or terrible situation. Death, for instance, even if it comes gently after a long and happy life, brings loss and grief to loved ones. When it is untimely, sudden or painful, through accident or illness, the shock, strain and heartache can be appalling. And even before death, life can be full of suffering and hardship.

Amazingly, many people face these things very well. How? Some are more courageous or optimistic than others. But it's not always about that, nor fatalism or mere stoicism. It can be a deep, abiding sense of peace among all the fear and uncertainty and pain.

For many people, the core of this is a relationship with God. Out of that comes the conviction and experience that God is bringing some good out of every human situation – including suffering – and that ultimately he will make sense out of it all.

We are often troubled, but not crushed; sometimes in doubt, but never in despair; there are many enemies, but we are never without a friend; and though badly hurt at times, we are not destroyed.

From 2 Corinthians 4

The real value of ease cannot be appreciated without having known pain, nor of sweetness without having tasted bitterness, nor of good without having seen evil, nor even of life itself without having passed through death.

Sadhu Sundar Singh

SECURITY

Understanding choice friendship

TRUST warmth

B·A·L·A·N·C·E LOVE

Happiness Accord Blessing

TRANQUILLITY

Freedom

MATURITY peace SURPRISE!

harmony

Zest cheer Enthusiasm

Joy C·A·L·M Life HONOUR

BLISS Delight

comfort pleasure QUIET

FRESHNESS TENDERNES

Laughter GROWTH fruition

HEALTH sunshine